PRESIDENTS OF THE UNITED STATES

American History For Kids
Children Explore History Book Edition

BABY PROFESSOR
EDUCATION KIDS

Speedy Publishing LLC
40 E. Main St. #1156
Newark, DE 19711
www.speedypublishing.com

BARACK OBAMA

is the 44th and current President
of the United States 2009 - present.
He is most famous for being the
first African American President
of the United States.

GEORGE W. BUSH

was the 43rd President of the United States from 2001 - 2008. Bush is the only president to have a Master of Business Administration (MBA) degree.

BILL CLINTON

was the 42nd President of the United States from 1993 - 2001. He is known for being president during one of the longest periods of peace and economic expansion in American history.

GEORGE H. W. BUSH

was the 41st President of the United States from 1989 - 1993. He was awarded the Distinguished Flying Cross medal while serving as a pilot in World War II.

RONALD REAGAN

was the 40th President of the United States from 1981 - 1989. During his military career he served in the U.S. Army Air Forces during WW2.

JIMMY CARTER

was the 39th President of the United States from 1977 - 1981. He was the first president to be born in a hospital.

GERALD FORD

was the 38th President of the United States from 1974 - 1977. nearly died in World War II when a typhoon hit his aircraft carrier and it caught fire.

RICHARD M. NIXON

was the 37th President of the United States from 1969 - 1974. He is known for ending the Vietnam War and improving U.S. relations with the Soviet Union and China.

LYNDON B. JOHNSON

was the 36th President of the United States from 1963 - 1969. At 6 feet 3 1/2 inches he was the second tallest president.

JOHN F. KENNEDY

was the 35th President of the United States from January 1961 until his assassination in November 1963. He was the first president who was a Boy Scout.

DWIGHT D. EISENHOWER

was the 34th President of the United States from 1953 - 1961.

HARRY S. TRUMAN

was the 33rd President of the United States from 1945 - 1953. He is most known for putting an end to World War II in the Pacific by dropping the atomic bomb on Japan.

FRANKLIN D. ROOSEVELT

was the 32nd President of the United States from 1933 - 1945. He was the first president to appear on television during a 1939 broadcast from the World's Fair.

HERBERT HOOVER

was the 31st President of the United States from 1929 - 1933. He did not accept his salary for president, but had it donated to charity.

CALVIN COOLIDGE

was the 30th President of the
United States from 1923 - 1929.
His real first name is John, which
he dropped in college.

WARREN G. HARDING

was the 29th President of the
United States from 1921 - 1923.
When he was younger he was
known by the nickname "Winnie".

WOODROW WILSON

was the 28th President of the
United States from 1913 - 1921. He
was the first president to visit
Europe while still in office.

WILLIAM HOWARD TAFT

was the 27th President of the United States from 1909 - 1913. At 332 pounds, Taft was the heaviest president in history.

THEODORE ROOSEVELT

was the 26th President of the
United States from 1901 - 1909.
At 42 years, 10 months, 18 days
old he was the youngest man to
hold the office of president.

WILLIAM MCKINLEY

was the 25th President of the United States from 1897 - 1901. He had a pet parrot named "Washington Post".

BENJAMIN HARRISON

was the 23rd President of the
United States from 1889 - 1893.
Some people called him the "human
iceberg" because he had such
a stiff personality.

GROVER CLEVELAND

was the 22nd and 24th President of the United States from 1885 - 1889 and 1893 to 1897. He was the only president to be married in the White House.

CHESTER A. ARTHUR

was the 21st President of the United States from 1881 - 1885. He reportedly had over 80 pairs of pants.

JAMES A. GARFIELD

was the 20th President of the United States, serving from March 4, 1881 until his assassination later that year. He was the first president whose mother attended his inauguration.

RUTHERFORD B. HAYES

was the 19th President of the
United States from 1877 - 1881. He
held the first Easter Egg Roll at
the White House which has become
an annual tradition.

ULYSSES S. GRANT

was the 18th President of the
United States from 1869 - 1877.
He is most known for being the
lead general of the Union troops
during the American Civil War.

ANDREW JOHNSON

was the 17th President of the United States from 1865 - 1869. He made his own clothes for much of his life.

ABRAHAM LINCOLN

was the 16th President of the
United States from 1861 - 1865. He
was known as a gifted storyteller
and liked to tell jokes.

JAMES BUCHANAN

was the 15th President of the United States from 1857 - 1861. He was the only president who never married.

FRANKLIN PIERCE

was the 14th President of the
United States from 1853 - 1857. He
was the first president to put a
Christmas tree in the White House.

MILLARD FILLMORE

was the 13th President of the United States from 1850 - 1853. Fillmore was one of the original founders of the University of New York at Buffalo.

ZACHARY TAYLOR

was the 12th President of the United States from 1849 - 1850. Taylor joined the army as a lieutenant and quickly rose in the ranks.

JAMES K. POLK

was the 11th President of the
United States from 1845 - 1849.
Polk added 1.2 million square miles
of land to the United States.

JOHN TYLER

was the 10th President of the United States from 1841 - 1845. He is known for being the first president to serve without being elected to office.

WILLIAM HENRY HARRISON

was the 9th President of the United States (1841). He was only president for one month before he died.

MARTIN VAN BUREN

was the 8th President of the
United States from 1837 - 1841. He
was the only president to speak
English as a second language.
His first language was Dutch.

ANDREW JACKSON

was the 7th President of the
United States from 1829 - 1837.
He is the only president to have
been a prisoner of war.

JOHN QUINCY ADAMS

was the 6th President of the
United States from 1825 - 1829.
Adams grew up during the time
of the American Revolution.

JAMES MONROE

was the 5th President of the
United States from 1817 - 1825.
He was the third president to
die on the 4th of July.

JAMES MADISON

was the 4th President of the United States from 1809 - 1817. His last words were "I talk better lying down."

CPSIA information can be obtained
at www.ICGtesting.com
Printed in the USA
LVHW060442150620
658073LV00017B/1242